In this book, I share my life's journey, deeply influenced and guided by a higher power. This divine presence has been a source of inspiration, granting me time and joy to explore and express my talent. It is a testament to the affirming and admirable impact of this spiritual guidance on my creative process.

I am pleased to dedicate this book to my mother, my unwavering pillar of strength and source of inspiration. Her indomitable spirit and encouragement have adorned me with courage and taught me to never set limits on my aspirations.

Hector Masekoameng

THE CHANGE OF FORMATION NEVER ENOUGH

AUSTIN MACAULEY PUBLISHERS™
LONDON • CAMBRIDGE • NEW YORK • SHARJAH

Copyright © Hector Masekoameng 2024

The right of Hector Masekoameng to be identified as author of this work has been asserted by the author in accordance with sections 77 and 78 of the Copyright, Designs and Patents Act 1988.

All rights reserved. No part of this publication may be reproduced, stored in a retrieval system, or transmitted in any form or by any means, electronic, mechanical, photocopying, recording, or otherwise, without the prior permission of the publishers.

Any person who commits any unauthorised act in relation to this publication may be liable to criminal prosecution and civil claims for damages.

A CIP catalogue record for this title is available from the British Library.

ISBN 9781398493070 (Paperback)
ISBN 9781398493087 (e-pub e-book)

www.austinmacauley.com

First Published 2024
Austin Macauley Publishers Ltd®
1 Canada Square
Canary Wharf
London
E14 5AA

I extend my heartfelt thanks to Austin Macauley Publishers for their dedication and professionalism throughout the publishing process. Lastly, I acknowledge my own journey in creating this work. Despite facing anxiety and pressure, I persisted, driven by a deep-seated vision and determination. This book is a testament to that perseverance.

The Hobo

The hobo, what's on your mind?
The hobo, what's on your imagination?
About controlling the cars.
Hobo, how do you find your spirit
Riveting between North, South, East and West?
The hobo, what's your knowledge?

Hobo, what's your knowledge?
Hobo, what's your knowledge?
The hobo, I will be admired to take some of your
Skills as my barely of dignity and pleasure.

Hobo, you are magic and majestic artistic and boldly at your talent.
Hobo, I give much of time trying to learn and be on your figure.

Hobo, you're artistic and boldly of you, it's brain storming
And your character is marvellous.
Hobo, your mind-set is a right sat prissy and pride.
Your light to me continues lighting to the fullest like a full moon at night.
Hobo, I will like to learn from you.

The Bluetooth

The Bluetooth
The Bluetooth
The Bluetooth
The Bluetooth

The Master Creation of Creatures
The Bluetooth, the Creative giver
The Bluetooth, the brew hand feeding Creatures
The brew hand to feed 'Creatures'
What meant for the stomach.
The Bluetooth, the giver and profounder of creatures.

The giver of creature
The giver of creature
The brew hand to giver, what meant for stomach
The Bluetooth, the brew reach for creatures and connection
The motion of wellbeing of life in motive and standard of life.

The Bluetooth, hanger can lead a motive and distress
But giving can desire on infinity of life and creation.
What is meant for such can meant for anything that lives
And knowing how to breathe in two state of life.

The Eye Wakeup by the Light

The eye wakeup by the light
The eye wakeup by the light
The eye wakeup by the light
The eye wakeup by the light

The leads of darkness never return
In the light, but the eye knows how
To open in the light. The shadow in the
Darkness, it's the profounder of the darkness.

The darkness and form of shadow
I am the light,
I evolve in the darkness to show life and way though.
Never fool me, never loose me, never loose
Faith in me
'I am the light'
I show the eye way through.

The Wait of Hider

The wait of hider
The wait of hider
The wait of hider
The wait of hider

The wait of conjecture
The work of conjecture life and balance need from progress.
The wait of conjecture, relation and powerful balance
The altitude and attitude of master of life.

The worst can change wellbeing of happiness into delightness
Of hardness of life, but the best conquer all of life.
All in different approach of life.

The Boy Who Was Hit by a Lightning

The boy and the lightning
The boy and the lightning
The boy and the lightning
The boy and the lightning

The lightning never allows the figure of emotion between
The boy, but the lightning always travels with the nature and nature
Decide the lightning to blaster with emotion to the boy.

The boy who was hit by a lightning
The boy always grieves to share emotion with the light, but
Always the lightning changes figures and profound character.

The easer the life of emotion that figured the boy to bear
Emotion with the lightning in some ways,
The bears figure with the essence of nature and its spirit.

The Change of Faces

The change of faces
The change of faces
The change of faces
The change of faces

The change of faces that alight emotion and bitterness
Face never lies it laws with emotion and sustainable of inwards
Between angry and smiling. The change of faces procrastinate
Between the face enlightenment and the flows of emotion.

Face proves encouragement and delight the favour with
Emotion and bitterness the laws between happiness and elaborate
Of angriness.
The change of faces
The change of faces
The change of faces
Reason with the bill of encouragement and
Evolve the endorsement in life.

Dream of Basis

The dream of basis
The dream of basis
The dream of basis
The dream of basis

Dream of basis it's enrolled by the vision, the rage
Bitter, through the elastic of consistent through darkness
Thrilling emotion and character of human being.

The dream of basis, why you're enlightened with memories but erase
The unwanted, it's minor and unruly to characterise between
You coming alive in an' consult mind only.

Dream of basis you enlighten me with spirit to hold on at
Any figure of life ahead on to you, you rule my life.

The Act of a Con Master

Art of a con master
Art of a con master
Art of a con master
Art of a con master

Con master the figure of art.
Art realises the beauty and the wellbeing life, you think I am talking about the thief of a con master or some of something? But well, you're not wrong or you may right, how so let's get to truth.

The art of con master.
The beauty of look in every phrase of look with a square side of vertical equal and side horizontal in every phrase of the corner of the eyes.

The look of con master always resend emotion at any relation of a yards at any meter's and direction.
The con master ament the attention at any laws of direction.
I still time and important of emotion and channel figure your eyes.

A Giant of Creature in Nature

Giant of creature in nature
Giant of creature in nature
Giant of creature in nature
Giant of creature in nature

Nature the treats of love, the energy
Drawer the feel treats of love.
The giant of creature in nature.

The nature infiltrate the spirit in me
The nature infiltrate the spirit in me
The nature in filtrate the spirit in me
Does it do the same with you? I am asking alongside

Be nature, be nature, be nature
Be love, be the giant of creature in nature

I Am the Roots

I am the roots
I am the roots
I am the roots
I am the roots

I am roots, I am the roots through the soil on
Solid hard surface, I grow on particular surface
I beauty the land with my nature.

I braw rich the affluent rich for then if is
Unreachable. I am the roots
I live under 'the tree' I am the heart of the tree.

I am unstoppable, even along your cut me on top
I will grow, I will survive, I will survive.

The Beast in Me

The beast in me
The beast in me
The beast in me
The beast in me

The beast in me always had droves in me.
The beast drove me for conquer at any compact that comes across in life (courage, spirit, limitless) nonstop keep up daily and night.

Beast drove me for huge relation and mechanical development me in spirit and mind. My occurrence and love that droves in me for change.

The beast in me droves me for change in my life.
The beast in me droves me for change in my character.
The beast in me droves me too hard to care to make it.
The beast in me droves me change in indifferent.

The beast in me journey

The Women of Rock

The women of rock
The women of rock
The women of rock
The women of rock

The women of mother lander
Women of creation, the creator of love
The rock of rock, mother of rock roof fender
Roof fender, the bender of air.

The mother, the mother
The mother, the mother
The mother, 'the lover', the lover', the uplift in love'
The creator, the lover.

The bender like for most like the tree through the roots.

The Mask

The mask
The mask
The mask
The mask

The mask, the invile and change looks for any attornment
of looks.
The invile and the attornment of looks.
I am the mask, I am the mask
(It's hard to look at me right).

The mask, I won't scare you, I will change your emotion
I am the mask
I will change your attributes and gain in control of you never
resend me.
I am your positive position.

Look, look, I am the mask, I am the mask feel my looks.
The mask

The Motion of Darkness in Life

The motion of darkness
The motion of darkness
The motion of darkness
The motion of darkness

The motion of life has figures of dark resents, 'clueless'
Unbarred and bitterness. The usually change are bar for
greatness in life. The motion of darkness.

The darkness won't change for the fact you got what it
Take for barley in your life, 'yah' I got it 'what it takes'
Are you?
Change the motion of darkness in life into the motion of lightness
After all you got what it takes and up for challenge.

Clueless, clueless, unbarred, unbarred, bitterness, bitterness
resents words.

The Limitation of Heart

The limitation of heart
The limitation of heart
The limitation of heart
The limitation of heart

The limitation of heart, the groom of heart
Uphold for big resents and bigger, biggest for what it takes.
Love 'joy' peaceful taker of any places.
Heart desires of love and floured.

The energy that resents perspective and glamour
The limitation of heart

The Positive Energy

The positive energy
The positive energy
The positive energy
The positive energy

The game changer any the source of
Positive garner at any compact of life.
Positive energy, lover, barley challenger.

The life challenger, they shall conger, they shall prosper
They mean to challenge negative to positive relation
(The work of positive energy)

Negative Energy

The negative
The negative
The negative
The negative

The negative relation between two
Relationship, hard core, minor between negative
and positive, it's an impact of figures.

The negative, the negative

Don't allow bitterness, 'native negative energy' enroll
You at currently what you have 'be master of roller'

Be being master and counter attack.

The negative
The negative

Lonely Guy

Lonely guy
Lonely guy
Lonely guy
Lonely guy

I am the lonely guy, wait the lonely
The lonely minded and spirit grabber
The lonely upper hand and master.
I am willow winner master factor.

Good attributor 'hard winner' hard winner
Minority, lonely hard work winner

I am lonely, I am lonely but winner.

Spirit Gainer

Spirit gainer
Spirit gainer
Spirit gainer
Spirit gainer

The spirit gainer, the attributor of
Energy and the gainer of spirit.
Gainer of spirit and spiritually.
The changer of motion 'the lender of directions in occasion.'

I am the spirit gainer
I am the spirit gainer

A Good Singer

The good singer
The good singer
The good singer
The good singer

The good singer, the browse of continuator
Good singer well developed and endeavour
The voice of splendour of each character
Endeavour and opener of ears

Endeavour the voice of vocal and equivocal
That profound location and inserts good character.
The good singer
The good singer

The good singer, the sound finder, the taker
To places, the locator of love, spirit, melancholy and prejudice of love.

The Voice That Never Dies

The voice that never dies
The voice that never dies
The voice that never dies
The voice that never dies

The voice of passion, love, clinical and hidden
The passion and demand the attention
Eager love intellect the fresh.

The voice of love that never dies
The voice of love that never dies
The voice of love that never dies

It's sweet love and bend with sets of adorable love.

The Football Lover

The football lover
The football lover
The football lover
The football lover

I love football, I love football,
Who love football, It's me "ARE YOU?"
Football lover, the love in roll in deep
It's predilection and major in big
Love.

The football lover
The football lover 'the attributes'
The deeper the connector of love.

The Chaser of Dreams

I am the chaser
I am the chaser
I am the chaser
I am the chaser

The chaser of dreams and predilection way
The love is hidden for what I love
Love for my dreams are precisely
Prescribed in love 'proper' aspects and aspiration.

I am a dreamer
I am a dreamer
I am a dreamer
I am a dreamer 'I FLOAT WITH WATER'
I am a dreamer
Chaser

I am the dreamer.

The Love of Books

The love of book, it's love
The love of book, it's love
The love of book, it's love
The love of book, it's love

The continuator of special treats
The influencer of love and hidden work
of beauty in me
Who's me?
I am in love with books.

I get love in a book, in predilection occasion of adornment
and hidden beauty in me
Who's me?

I love books, I love books, I love books
Mainly attender in every motives of books.

A Hard Worker

The hard worker
The hard worker
The hard worker
The hard worker

I am the hard worker the bender.
The bender of hard motion on any occasion
Attribute.

The hard worker of love
The hard worker of love
The hard worker of love, he is a hard worker.
Love of work and creation aspect, aspiration to create love.

The passion in hard working.

The Innocent Boy

The innocent boy
The innocent boy
The innocent boy
The innocent boy

Love grows in me, I grow like a tree
Love grows in me, I grow
To love more, live long
I am innocent.

My innocent draws attention
My innocent draws love
My innocent draws precocious and inflict insurable
Hidden beauty and love that never perish.

The Charmer

The charmer
The charmer
The charmer
The charmer

Look, look, I am charmer
I am beauty, I am adorable
Beauty love me 'me too' I love
Beauty and the beauty love me.

I am charmer
I am charmer
Young kindly looks of a young beauty rabbit, after born.

I am charmer, I draw attention with love

The God Lover

The god lover
The god lover
The god lover
The god lover

The god lover figure of situation mighty all
In any situation, the uprising of darkness.
The god lover any particular.
The changer for manifold holes at any character during
Compact of any for most of life.

The god 'fearer' the bisector of world in between ways,
The changer motive. 'God of lover' good in loving.
The god, the bender, the bender of cluster.

The god vile and expressly of determination, unilateral for any change of life.

(The god, the bless for all)

The Love in Me

The love in me
The love in me
The love in me
The love in me

The love in me unrated.
Your find good simples and good loving
Of love joy and untitled for unity creation.

My love in me, it's for build.
My love in me, it's for build.
My love in me, it's for joy and creation.

The love in me is unconstitutional at clock of a tick
In every moment joy colourfully and bend with strong personality.
Love for me is passion, greedy and untitled
For what 'I love' I meant to have it fore ever.

(The love me)

The Lion Inside the Boy

The lion inside the boy
The lion inside the boy
The lion inside the boy
The lion inside the boy

The lion the wild of creature that lived for long
Inside the boy (for life and worst there is a pure pull
Through, along if water can turn into solid, but it will
openly change into liquid state).

The boy changed, for 'no' change only the spirit of a
Lion gained through the blood arteries.
Transmitted and profound the wealthy onto his mind
and spiritually.

Boy became a cluster of himself to combine the life of a
Creature and the life of a human being particularly to have
Huge life change. Moment of the boy and the lion.

The Work of Art

The work of art
The work of art
The work of art
The work of art

The art in love, I am the art
Good proper of aspect of love, the attentive in any condition.

The leaner proper attributer and attender of love in every direction.

I am the art of joy, spirit, every giver
The messenger of massage
The founder of hidden predilection occasion.

THE END